# A SLEEVE OF BLUE

# *A Sleeve of Blue*

## Margaret Roncone

Goldfish Press • Seattle, Washington

Published by
Goldfish Press, an imprint of Chrysanthemum Publications, Inc.

ISBN 13: 978-1950276-22-6
ISBN 10: 1-950276-22-8
Library Congress Control Number: 2022949047

Cover art: Sandra Noel
Book design: Russel Davis, Gray Dog Press

Goldfish Press is a literary press of all genres.

Goldfish Press
4545 42nd Avenue SW, Suite 211
Seattle, WA 98116

Website: goldfishbooks.com

*We return to the wild again and again*
*despite our hearts caged in bone.*

—m.r.

*for Lucille—whose feet left earth too soon.*

# Contents

# A Sleeve of Blue

## *Ritual*

every morning I wash the dust of night from my eyes. i still see
my hip bones while lying on my back. these are handles the world
holds onto when teaching me a lesson. why dahlias continue to
bloom in autumn. why the mouth of god remains open. why
the earth softens when feet are bare. and my prayer plant's hands
lifting at dusk…is this an answer too?

### *Unknown Bird Calls*

I lean towards the green
right ear of indelible song

between lie peonies,
wild poppies defying
wind's gravel play

soft hoof prints
stencil paths to the woods

here deer sleep
in swirls of tall grass,
bedded while our dreams
capture lives past.

## Middle of August

I have yet to find a 4-leaf clover among dance driven dandelions.
Burnt grass abounds. No measure or map for our lives but the
shortening of days. Hot spells come and go as we take cover in
nightshade plants. Farm stands with limitless trust jar profits sit
on steady tables. Fragrant herbs, yellow pimply squash, sturdy
weighted cucumbers. I gather promised good of neighbors' labor
and find home again and again.

### We Plant Our Fathomless Lives

We plant our fathomless lives
on the dark side of the moon.
I invent new words (vowel less)
with the tap of a pen.
If I squeeze my eyes together
I'm in tall grass bowing to the sea.
Uninformed about rowboats,
trusting no one with an oar
no matter the vessel.
Preferring sails to motors
I take deep breaths,
practice non-religion.
After 2 a.m. strangers appear
with snowman faces
throw a stone at them;
they'll disappear

## Weather (1)

Today wind stalks rain
Or is it the other way around?
When I think of this happening
as the earth tips its axis
I get lightheaded.
When I photograph rain
it appears as snow.
I'm on a stage with angels
trimming their wings;
wind forms green caverns in a cedar –
a thousand mouths opening.
I listen but all I hear
Is the stage floor creaking.

(another version previously appeared in *Goose River Anthology*)

## Quest

I visit a spiritual shop
to find my mission

a religion of cream stucco;
Spanish moss

a place to search and rescue
my floundering soul

a small Buddha statue perhaps,
a flapping string of prayer flags

a lifeboat of possibilities

my head filled with
lingering incense

of doomed fate

my tongue
forms the word
*calm*

I hear my floppy heart say *wish*.

## What She Sees from Here

Sea roughened by wind
a battered sky hung above
thin skin of fog
scarring the mountain

on the street
a small boy

mother hanging on to him
by his backpack

angry words bounce
off the sidewalk

young boy clutches
a bag of candy
notices nothing

bus hisses by

## Perhaps

perhaps the new moon is
hanging her feet too low
in our cloud mottled sky

or my mother has turned
over in her grave
now I'm meditating
instead of praying

I have no rosaries
nor holy water
if I did I'd braid the beads
through my hair

use holy water
to soak my
swollen fingers

perhaps then I would
find the secret door
to heaven
hidden in the garden floor
covered with pulled brown weeds
tales I passed down
to my children
told to me
by my grandmother

under the cherry tree

under the cherry tree
where my grandfather tried to fix
the engine of his angry heart.

## Trust in a Universe

Not everything holds tenderness

white lights glow on a Christmas tree
with upturned needles

in the produce aisle I forgive myself
mangoes traveled distance

here an alley divides us
from small commerce
I drink my tea
study trees holding back light.

## Untitled

I'm waiting for pounding to end
glass against brick
empty bottle grazing a wire fence
by a bully on the playground
awaiting his next victim

I know it's my blood
navigating for the right channel
in a brain gone haywire

somewhere beyond throbbing
a bird quivers a branch of song.

## Strange Day

cave drawings
on my lips
instead of a kiss

I voice my insecurity
send it off
on a sailing ship

shore at high tide
a rough spot
to land

perhaps it's
pure luck

I have a hat rack
to scan my restless brain

a room full
of moths
to distract me.

## *Untitled*

A woman now dead once told me I have beautiful feet. You refer
to our untended grass as 'lawn'. I cringe and think 'suburban
sprawl'. What we narrowly escaped from. I repeat in my head
'grass' 3 times, waving dust motes skyward with both hands. Our
resident robin pecks gravel knowing you've done a fine job cutting
deer's midday meal. South Sudan no rain.   Women raped for war's
reason. Babies turn wide brown eyes to dried breasts. Hot skies
burn grasslands. Thieves of night steal young girls. What have we
not done? Countries are peeling off the map of Africa. You clean
the tangled green strands from wet mower blades. Open the sturdy
door to view evening news.

## *Untitled*

The ocean floor brims with footprints. Once the fish were us. Now we are them. Soft lungs replace flapping gills. We lack the magic of stars' navigation. Leave the butter knife at the side of your plate. The flesh is ripe with forgiveness. Dreams of water resolve the fires of night. The shore a distant table, a floating feast.

(previously appeared in *Three Birds Dreaming*)

## *Watchful*

A hundred years
between then and now

How many ferries
cross watery hearts

A gardener chooses
her glorious peony

The moon pins it on
blue bosom morning

I watch from a
distant star

twine a shiny wreath
of early light.

## Weather (2)

Wind cleaned them all
small towns,
married fields of
oats and barley

you'd think someone would notice
stop signs with their silly red grins
little boys and girls holding hands
dancing in circles;
cow paths rich with stink
how they disappear
one after another
factory closures
families standing by roadsides
suitcases in sweaty hands.

There was weather
or was it my imagination
storms rumbling into town
like a band of refugees
take cover    find shelter
the willow with it's
no's and yes's
shaking its head in the
lunatic wind
voices in my head
words without vowels
where do we imprint our hands;
who can we follow?
without a voice in the
cave of swimmers,
those lovely swimmers
hanging on to sandstone
swollen bellies; fin-like feet.

## *Please Drop Your Nickels In The Slot*

The one you find
in the eye of the needle
between stratus clouds
and the great beyond;
listen to the battling rain
against your window

you asked for this
but the universe is
at your command

my mind is a nuthatch
my fingers grow
as the moon
waxes and wanes
hush hush
don't give it
a name
or it will come true.

## Imagine

The first time I saw a fox it was trotting confidently across a police station parking lot. The same morning a man stepped in front of a commuter train. Apron of grass flattened. Somewhere in Chicago someone was emptying coffee grounds down a drain. I hoped wakening starlings sky bound wouldn't form black ribbons. I kept smelling something burning. Smoke rose between commuters departing the train. The world once survived on orchards and vineyards, an occasional slaughtering held over a forgotten holiday. Imagine the signalman being there. Imagine mourning doves lined up on a telephone wire, silent.

## Picking Raspberries

I'm ambidextrous
no matter what hand is given

the basket fills
with plump fruit

the nuns never tried
to change me
from left to right
despite
the fairy tales of
wicked witches
hiding deep
in the forest
cauldrons boiling
atop an open fire

I was predicted to be a queen
my land was sold to the highest bidder

in the back row I frantically
flailed my hand
no nun noticed

no one pays attention
to women who's lives
float between planets
searching for an
uninhabited
star.

## John the Baptist

ate locusts and wild honey
I drink the lake
with my eyes
later with every pore
I am a sunflower at
sunrise
a desert at first
rainstorm
a widow whose husband
suddenly appears
after war
sand in my eyes
I see clearly
I'm looking for a man
with a round face
a woman with a wedge haircut
neither prophet nor poet
only someone I know
who knows someone
Here is a stone
at the bottom of the lake
you give me –
granite, white stripes
like the clouds barely
sketching sky
I slip between my breasts
a talisman to carry through
the cold waters to the dock
older now
we walk the slippery stones
to the deep
where unfamiliar round faces
disguise as rocks.

## Sometimes

a jar of heaven's bouquet greets me at wakening. sometimes a jolt
from hell's back door. this early morning a banshee cry from my
lips.   an animal in heat. my knees were closed my wide mouth
open as the 'A' in Autumn.   the neighbor thought she heard a
tree cracking before hitting dry ground. I tell her get used to it.
my soul roams most nights with a butterfly net. blankets wrapped
around me like east coast heat. I have shed the domesticity of day.
my body frozen in place by old fear. look how it turns my eyes
gray. look how my fingers cease trembling as dusk appears.

## *Autumn Light*

lengthening shadows
discard bright light
store it in a
cupboard for next June

what I notice and
pause to study
are narrators of
a fresh story
unfolding in pebbled gravel
dried grass
and moon's play on stone.

## *Longing*

I could be in a desert
thirsty for pilgrims' rain

clouds strapped to a
darkening sky

moon lights a map
of archipelagos

blue streams garnish
a multitude of possibilities
spaces between clouds
have all the answers

to every religious mystery
my scrappy soul longs for.

### Untitled

*—for Sandra*

Clouds pass like
dark birds
  losing flight
a friend's heartbreak
will be carried
  by many hands
but who will mend the tear?

## *Our Country*

take those hairline fractures
below earth's crust
it's not primal disease
it's something worse

highway metal's thrust
will not protect you
neither will billowing bags

give me air balloons
with colorfast dreams attached
so we may exit through a black hole

if we're lucky the floating wall
of smog will do
its dirty laundry work first
hold your breath child of wonder.

## *Homage*

How to honor you
 o hue blue
you blind my eyes
with blissfulness
If I were a burning star
I would light your cigarette
watch you inhale
and turned the world red.

## Resolutions

to swim upstream navigating by the stars
to know the Sitka from the pinion
the sadness from the grief

more often, to feel the wind against bare skin
to satisfy my yearning for the sea

to seek the frenzy of cicadas, night birds,
tree frogs

every 15 hours
to enter triumphant sleep.

## The Rosary Worn Around Her Neck
—for Rosanne

crucifix hung at her missing breast
we met in a shop where neither
one of us could afford the clothes
the boiled wool coat eyed with lust
colorful silk scarves around
cold-eyed mannequins
she from the East coast
as was I
both offered a body part
for salvation
her smiling face now a halo
angels hold in billowy cloud.

## Still

I carry my father's face above my shoulders floating like a raft. A piece of antler tears the sky as an old woman slowly walks a dog. I watch her, one eye closed to the sea of memory and mansions. Maybe in my craving for sustenance I strangely resemble someone else. The reflection in the mirror is a different child whose sunhat sits akimbo. See how lips work without speaking. It is a star's desire to nest in the cradle of heaven.

## *Untitled*

I will begin here
where the orchard ends
build a stone wall
assuming weather
holds up the sky

red poppies grow well
in gravel
I will fill a sack in Autumn with spent seeds
small birds will envy my life
and I theirs for flight.

*I fall in love with a photo of e. e. cummings in a new yorker magazine while in the waiting room of an ophthalmologist's office*

it's black and white
he's looking intently
away from the camera at
a parade of lower case 'i's
a hyphened world
linear time and rhyme
disappear in a desert
of white stallions
my eyes balloon
at handsome
I need to nestle in his
supra sternal notch
feel his swallows
as they gather
on telephone wires
stretched
from limb
to beautiful limb

## Date Three

with eyes dip-sticked in the Caribbean
you tell me your flying dream;
ask me to sew the flag of Alaska with you
say "Big Dipper in shimmer gold thread"

we've only had three dates but I already know
your dad's pick up is white;
sits in a Texan oil field waiting for you
we share history of making
butter in a Mason jar;
your head sideways when
hearing the muffler of a '79 Chevy
heading towards you down the road,
your dad's foot on the gas, your small hands gripping the wheel

our first meeting at Green Lake
you asked me to remove my sunglasses
so you could see my eyes;
our last date at Pike Place Market
I reluctantly let you snap a photo
of me with your phone,
farm trucks rumbling in the background

in some foreign dictionary there's
a word for this,
a word I do not know.

## The Visit

Lucy takes the lavender,
places it next to a holy card
with Madonna and Child;
a small bowl of loose change,
a miniature painting of a white poodle.

Her room is gray, matted with
the light of dusk.
Her eyes, knotted with love,
search for something familiar.
Hummingbird feeder outside her window
attracts wasps –
hospital food tangled with
raspberry bushes she picked
gnarl her sleep.
Her sister returns home,
cooks fresh herbs,
wildflower honey in the pantry awaits tea,
down pillow on bed,
dreams of Lucy walking again.

## Parish Life

a lover once told me I walk like a nun
all those hours at the blackboard
Sister Josette metering the day
with wooden pointer in hand

the damage of long division
multiplied by
confessional procession
our sins laying
stonework for schoolyard walls

'*red rover    red rover*
*please    let someone come over*'

a forest of hooded angels
votive candles circling
the willow in our yard
became my room

for a long time
I had little to say
I found myself by water,
whittled a pencil from a branch
wrote in the sand
x over you = z.

### Still looking for Missouri

your quarters stacked
on the nightstand
like a pile of spent moons
all but 11 states represented

after every errand
a shuffle of silver
patiently waiting
for the missing to appear

I think of you
as a young boy;
did you collect nickels
hoping for the magical buffalo?

## Miles at Sea

miles at sea
the lighthouse a blink in the
eye of the great white

years ago I had you
tied to a floating dock;
I wet my eyes daily
with salt water,
tears came easy
not for you
but for thousands who would
never know your lazy walk;
your hands
holding two worlds

paths through woods
twisted our hearts
and disentangled a frayed rope;
sandy embankment,
no foothold.

## Passing

Crows go about crow business,
miniature monks they are with
arrogant side glances,
beaks, tiny picks plucking
what is buried deep.
My mother's voice
through a thin glass shield of gray
what secrets did you take to the grave?
I watch your body as evening
brushes with cat raised back
slowly you turn your grey head left
a dying blossom seeking
the last of days' light
your face asymmetrical;
left eye still with constant stare
a bird's eye no longer seeking
branch nor prayer only
permission to imagine wings;
permission to ascend.

## The Father as Artist

Tell me again how your father instructed you into the language of food
how you   his first daughter   learned to balance an egg
on morning's shifting edge

learned mustard was a color to
shade the sky and side of trees
cream   a luxury found in stealing glances
a neighbor woman pruning roses
an ankle teased beneath her dress

tell me again how your father spoke without anger
stood at the window   watched
as the winter moon rose like the silver dollar stolen
from your grandfather's nightstand

he placed it in your hand
told you to trust your instincts
with strange men
never leave questions unanswered like an open door.

## High Tide

You were not the same after
the shoelaces unknotted everything
you held dry at high tide

You believed ravens crushed
the souls of night watchmen
under their wings

you had the world convinced
of a false hood
you carried a fistful of
shattered mirror

the blood you drew
from you those pale thin arms
was anemic, still blue.

(previously appeared in Three Birds Dreaming)

## *The Haywire Moon*

the same moon hanging
above flapping prayer flags
where I would
see your face
in dark reflection
of a window
wonder if you
remembered
the small stoned beach
where we talked
our differences
our opposing maps
of family, politics
everything
but the weight
of love.

## Red

offering pomegranate
you tell me
on first meeting you hoped
my face would be a face you could love
I eat the seeds, same jewel red
as the tulips
sitting between us
dipping tender-layered heads
towards the chestnut grain of table
like deer pausing for drink
unmistakable grace of nature
swollen repeated.

On the other side
of these panes of glass
pine trees scrub the sky
as ravens fly; suddenly perch,
monk robes gathered close
bearing witness to flight,
I imagine my bones hollowing
a soft wind sighing through a reed;
my glass eyes fixed on the moon
groaning with leftover light.

## Spider Season

My mother called October spider season
she took no notice of the patterns of nature,
playing cards and how they lined up in front
of her magnified eyes were high priority

it's September, spiders hang like small
crabs from porch crevices;
yellow moths scan late summer air.
Are they all victims of a hidden web's clutch?

Most of my childhood was misunderstood;
shadows of my young self lost on
street corners line my mind;
I sit with them on porch steps
while I savor a full moon in all it flavors;
my belly groans its loss.

## Hurry My Sweet

Everything rushes here
the leaves
darkness between

'*hurry my sweet*'

let me pin your favorite brooch
on your red wool coat

streetcars will stop for you
stars will spin on pink toe shoes

the widower's cheeks
will blush with delight

I will wait
shrouded in
sea's startling charm

my feet numbed by cold
wet sand.

## Black-Capped Chickadees and Homemade Pasta

As chickadees fling themselves from bare-budded branch,
I mound two cups of flour on the counter; make nest for 3 eggs,
first work the dough with fork, then hands find the right consistency;
a tablespoon of added water.

The chickadees read the arrival of Spring with acrobats
I sense the readiness of dough through fingers,
as mason bees emerge from white straws.

I remember my grandmother at her table,
flour up to her elbows
grandfather grumbling something
about boiled potatoes.

The years somersault by,
our list of desires grows smaller;
a gas-fired stove, a garden of cobbled stone,
our arms still reaching for each other.

## Blogger

I know a blogger named Ms. Moon
whom I've never met
and most likely never will.
She lives in Florida surrounded by chickens,
grandchildren and a lovely husband
with a beard who repairs
and rides scooters.
I study the picture of him
standing on a mattress with
scooter parts hanging like
mobiles above him.
Ms. Moon posts photos of
flowers in ceramic jars,
interesting pots and on this earth
she wears aprons and honesty,
for not wanting to make
pickles today but making them anyway.
She lines the jars
up on her table;
I want to take the next
train to Florida, borrow one of her aprons
and make pies.

*Three Women*

## Sophie

She remembers hearing "head for the hills", maybe an old Western
maybe her father's idea of escape from a bad marriage. When the
last of winter's snow turned as drab gray as a business suit and the
returning swallow built nests in the old widow's steepled roof, she
packed her rucksack with goat cheese wrapped in parchment, a
sewing kit, an old photo of Doris Day. She headed, well, you know
where. Wild dogs met her in the foothills. Took her three moon
cycles to get her voice tuned to the pack.

## Marcy

Laces her shoes with old rawhide, pulls thin arms through her
grandfather's worn pea coat. Screen door covered with moth wings
slams behind as she sneezes seven times, makes a wish. Checks the
hen house for fox tracks, punctured eggs. The lunar cycle marks
the tempo of her slow heaven. Every Thursday 3 a.m. walks the
shore of the pond, insomnia gripping like teeth of a mad dog.
Water hyacinth brush her bare legs. She remembers the cat lost last
Spring, how with her nearby, she never felt lonely. Marcy speaks
Creole, the hills answer with snow, a tree falling in the night,
sound of ribs cracking.

**Evangeline**

Knows black goes well with lace, wishes her legs were as long
as Rita Hayworth's. Her women friends think she's shallow, but
Evangeline knows the importance of identity. She has dreams
of being a trapeze artist, dyeing her hair blonde with pale green
stripes. Every morning she fine combs her lashes until they look
like apostrophes. Gives her hair 100 strokes with a boar bristle
brush, walks to church wearing wet boots. "Penance" she mutters
four times, crosses herself with pond water. She's content sleeping
alone, rubs olive oil along each limb, silk sheets beneath her, head
still to prevent wrinkles. Remembers the sound of her mother's old
mangle, re-checks the burn scar on her forearm. In the morning,
Evangeline brews coffee for one, feigns interest in the New York
Times, swallows two diet pills with her O.J. Her neighbor's old
pick-up, tires watermarked with salt water has her thinking about
leaving.

## Language is a Flame

I burn rosebuds
bergamot
to find
the birthplace
of my grandmother
who understood sorrow,
nylons wrapped
around ankles
potatoes boiling
on an ancient stove
a man who misunderstood
even the food
she placed before him
nothing warm enough
soft enough
only the wreck of a car
sitting useless
under the ancient cherry tree.

## The Cellar

Sorting nails at 4 a.m.
you find no words
to fill baby food jars
only dialect of metal on metal
a small mouth cap
your tongue refuses
the glue to seal your
letter to the outside world
you feed the hissing fire
with last years downed orchard
the slanted porch heaves
with gathering rain
this is how one man
rules his castle
a moat filled with drowning lovers
waiting the outstretched hand
how easily we bleed under the nail.

## Cape Breton

It was a graceful departure
the three day old moon rehearsed.
Hung in the leftover dawn
like a Chinese lantern,
abandoned by myriads of white robed maidens
waltzing across Orion.
Dawn swallowed her with a waking yawn.
I nearly missed the faded
grey eye of rounded light
still and watchful for morning.

## Untitled

The family next door is French,
mother feeds her 3 children lentils
for lunch,
serves rose hip tea in her garden to everyone…

Between the two yards grow peonies,
scented geranium, ground cover with purple haze…

In my sketchbook is a drawing
of her profile,
she is dreaming of the crab apple tree in
a French field,
miniature horses and children eating
bruise less fruit.

## Still Life

still on the tracks
plank-stretched steel
crossbows of veiny wood
stained red
like the dark star
leaving cold night
some lost soul tethered
his scrap of eternity here
sky staring down
her wide gray of noon
while among stones and gravel
his soft wounds were
laid to rest
across our path
he intersected our lives
between Cicero and Clyde
his last sound heard
metal on metal
vibrating through the
alley of his bones
his listless blood feeding
his final harvest of thought
between ashes to ashes
lies the bitter pain
I long to know he
listened to the
mourning doves' song
before they echoed his name

## My Unabridged Heart

My unabridged heart and I are one,
agree to leave the dawn unsavored.

Place 3 ripe pears on the side porch
for the starlings

pack light     3 matches, an abandoned beehive, 1 gold coin with
    fountain history

I remember the ghost singing in the closet,
the Sikh procession he promised on our journey.

Saffron robes wrap sun smashed tiled streets;
city gates off in the distance promise silk dancers at midnight.

A small fortune awaits us,
a barter of howling dogs for the peacock's feather eye.

## Old Truck Returns Home for Lunch

Gravel dust pitched up like hay in a big barn. sturdy old hands grasp steering wheel. Stella the dog sits in the passenger seat like the steady aging wife. truck sputters, coughs, backs up into bared grass. even the weeds are gone. stones spatter under worn leather boots. dog takes quick pee. stairs creak with determined weight.

## Katya and Arthur at Sevilla Train Station

a keyhole of desire is an open bed
they lie in rain
she huddled to his heavy frame

they agree to leave in the morning
head west to Cadiz

she a student of photography
he of freight trains;
a vagabond's web of survival

they brave open roads
for another city of blood oranges
eat nothing

his boots strapped with stories
her hair the nest he remembers from childhood

how they clung to the hips of nearby hills
how each desired dust and what lingers with it
gold, flour, salt,
tales of witches who sink to the bottom of the sea

near the city gates,
a pack of boxer dogs,
there's a small chance the procession will begin with them.

## I'm Going to Moscow

to trudge through deep snow
I will continue until
steeple clocks
stop chiming.
I will wear
scratchy shirts,
read Tolstoy,
find his orchard;
take a bite from
a wormy apple
offer the rest to a sleigh driver
in a topcoat,
his red worn hands
at the reins of
a horse I will steal.

### Travel Uncontained

what year was it I traveled to France with you? we lodged with
a friend in an old stone farmhouse. she with an orchard. fallen
apples and truffles found at the foot of a tree. her husband spoke
little English so was quiet. she talkative and laid fruit and cheese
after every meal. I still have the lime green placemats bought at the
farmers' market. taste of plums still on my tongue.

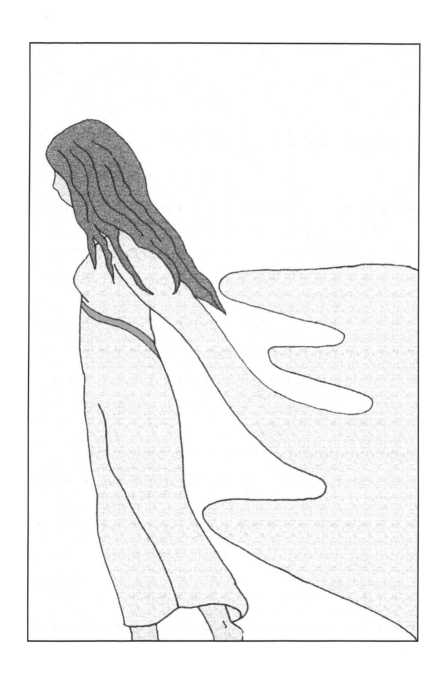

## About the Author

Margaret Roncone's poetry has appeared in *Chrysanthemum* and *Goose River Anthology*, and been published in *Three Birds Dreaming* with two other poets. On-line her work can be found in *Barnwood International Poetry Journal*, *Avocet*, and *Poets Against War*. Her poetry was performed as part of the Pierce College 10-minute Play Festival and was chosen for Seattle City Council's Wordsworth Program. She curated an open mic in Seattle for ten years, on Vashon Island for two years, and was facilitator for a poetry series at Chief Seattle Club. She lives on Vashon Island where frequent forest walks keep her inspired.

Made in the USA
Monee, IL
10 January 2023